LEARN T...

COLLECTION 9

Vowel Reference Card
Dolch Stories Only

Written by Mary Schuler
Illustrated by Nicholas Torres

Collection 9: This is a collection of five Dolch stories that builds on the previous collections by adding <u>Dolch Vowel Reference Card</u> words. In this collection, instead of only short vowel sounds and the long vowel sounds formed when a "silent e" is added to the end of the word, all the rest of the vowel sounds on the Vowel Reference Card will be used. All five stories are written with the *Dolch phonetic Sight Words. Each story will have a list of vocabulary words at the beginning as well as questions to answer at the end.

*The 315 Dolch Sight Vocabulary list is taken from the Picture Word Cards and Popper Words Set 1 (included in item #0-07-609422-7), plus Popper Words Set 2 (#0-07-602539-X) published by SRA (1-888-SRA-4543 or SRAonline.com).

NEXT BOOK

Collection 10: This is a collection of five more Dolch stories written with the <u>DOLCH Vowel Reference Card</u> words. Each story will have a list of vocabulary words at the beginning as well as questions to answer at the end.

DEDICATION

These books were created for children to help them learn how to read by using phonics skills systematically. These books are dedicated to parents, giving them an early literacy practical guide with tools.

ACKNOWLEDGMENTS

These books were created for _Schuler Phonics CORE (Second Part)_, authored by Mary M. Schuler. This collection includes Companion Stories #38-42.

It is highly recommended that BEFORE reading this book, your child/student should study the following sections in Schuler Phonics CORE (Second Part) Vowel Reference Card by Mary M. Schuler:

1. Single Consonants with Short Vowels
2. The FLOSS and CK Rule
3. Adding s and 's to nouns and verbs
4. Blends with Short Vowels
5. Digraphs with Short Vowels
6. Adding es to nouns ending s, x, z, ch, or sh
7. The Silent e Rule.
8. Compound Words and
9. Vowel Reference Card

www.parentreadingcoach.org
FOR TRAINING VIDEOS

Schuler Phonics and Companion Books WHERE "Sound it out" really works!

But to help it work, note the following:

Any word *italicized*/*underlined* in these stories should NOT be sounded out --- because sounding out just won't work on those words! (The words, "The" and "the" will not be italicized/underlined even though considered "non-phonetic"; there are just too many of them, and they really are not a problem!)

IMPORTANT for Collection 9: One sound but more than one letter (ea, au, aw, al, all, ai, ay, ee, igh, oa, ow, ew, oo, ar, or, er, ir, ur, oy, oi, ou) will be typed in **bold** in the words in these stories to help parents/students spot those vowel reference card sounds.

All of these words can be sounded out using the Vowel Reference Card!

Joseph's Vowel Reference Card

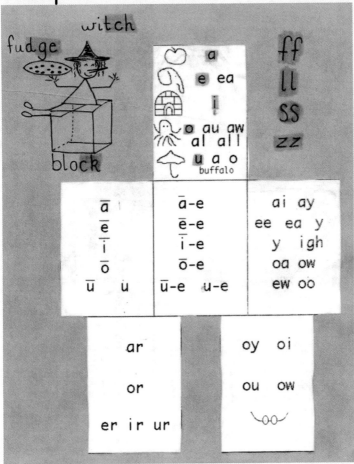

NOTE: Do you see the Silent e sounds right in the middle of the Vowel Reference Card? What do the a, e, i, o, and u say there?

NOTE: Now, single a, e, i, o, u do not just say the short vowel sound but also could say the long vowel sound. The letters a and o, also, have a third sound. Can you find all those sounds for a, e, i, o, and u?

NOTE: ea, ow, oo and y each have two sounds. Can you find those two sounds for each one?

It is highly recommended that BEFORE reading this book, you, parents, should watch the training video, Deep Dive, on www.parentreadingcoach.org, while viewing Joseph's Reading Review Column (next page).

It is highly recommended that BEFORE reading this book, you, parents should practice with your child the word lists provided by having your child:

1) circle the vowel sound from the vowel reference card;

2) say the vowel sound; and

3) read the word.

Repeat until mastery is reached.

Example

aim
and
ask
bake
bank
bat
bead
beck
beg
bent
big
bit
blank
blind
blow
book
bath
boy
brand
breast
bring
brown
bug
bum
but
came
cap
cart

For the stories in this collection your child should learn the following underlined/italicized words and parts of words by sight (Do NOT sound out --- It doesn't work!):

are	_horse/shoes_	_said_
bird/_house_	_house_	_school_
boat/_house_	_house_/sat	_shoe_
buy	_house_/sit	_shoes_
come	in/_to_	_should_
comes	_know_	_some_
could	_laugh_	_some/one_
_do_	_laughs_	_some_/thing
does	light/_house_	_some_/time
done	_live_ (short i)	_some_/what
door	no/_where_	_some/where_
eye	_of_	thank-_you_
eyes	_once_	the
farm/_house_	_one_	_their_
full	**out**/_come_	_there_
give	play/_house_	_they_
goes	_please_	_to_
green/_house_	_pull_	_two_
have	_put_	_u/pon_
horse	road/_house_	_walk_
horse/shoe	round/_house_	_want_

x

<u>warm</u>   <u>where</u>   <u>you</u>

<u>watch</u>   <u>who</u>   <u>your</u>

<u>watch</u>es   <u>work</u>

<u>were</u>   <u>would</u>

All the other words can be sounded out as they are
based on short vowel and single consonant, blend,
and digraph words, silent e rule, compounds, plus
Vowel Reference Cards words.

IMPORTANT NOTE FOR PARENTS/TEACHERS:

A or **a** should NOT be pronounced as long a (/ā/ as in the word say) in the phrase/sentence such as, "**A** Boy's and Girl's Show," or "Go up **a** tree." Instead, **A** or **a** should be pronounced as a short u (/ŭ/ as in umbrella /ŭ/ or up /ŭ/).

The e in the words **The** or **the** should NOT be pronounced as long e (/ē/ as in the word bee) in the phrase/sentence such as "**The** Toy Train," or "Don't try to hurt **the** bear." Instead the e in **The** or **the** should be pronounced as a short u (/ŭ/ as in umbrella /ŭ/ or up /ŭ/).

CONTENTS

STORY 1: DOLCH SIGHT WORDS

Black and Brown Bears

IMPORTANT: Before studying this vocabulary with your child and before having your child read the story note the following:

This is the first Companion Book to use the Vowel Reference Card words. Up to this point only the non-phonetic Dolch words have been marked in the stories (<u>*underlined and italicized*</u>). Now, however, the Vowel Reference Card teams will be marked in **bold** to help you, parents, help your children spot those vowel teams and <u>**refer them to the Vowel Reference Card**</u> to figure out their sound(s) and therefore be able to read the words.

(Note: The Vowel Reference Card is in the very back of this book!!!)

The single letters a, e, i, o, u, and now also y will not be marked at all as usual. However, parents, for example, if your child sees a single letter o in a word, like in dog, or go, or from, your child needs to be made aware that there are three possible sounds for that letter o (<u>**refer them to the Vowel Reference Card**</u>), not just octopus /ŏ/ as it has been up to this point! This is true for the single letters a (three possible sounds), e (two possible sounds), i (two possible sounds), u (three possible sounds), and y (two possible sounds). Silent e sounds still will not be marked in any way.

COMPANION STORY 38
DOLCH SIGHT WORDS

Non-phonetic Dolch sight words:
(<u>*underlined /italicized as usual*</u>)

<u>are</u>	in/<u>to</u>	thank-<u>you</u>
bird/<u>house</u>	light/<u>house</u>	the
boat/<u>house</u>	<u>live</u> (short i)	<u>their</u>
<u>come</u>	no/<u>where</u>	<u>there</u>
<u>could</u>	<u>of</u>	<u>they</u>
<u>do</u>	<u>one</u>	<u>to</u>
<u>door</u>	out/<u>come</u>	<u>walk</u>
<u>eye</u>	play/<u>house</u>	<u>want</u>
<u>eyes</u>	road/<u>house</u>	<u>where</u>
farm/<u>house</u>	round/<u>house</u>	<u>would</u>
<u>give</u>	<u>should</u>	<u>you</u>
green/<u>house</u>	<u>some</u>	<u>your</u>
<u>house</u>	<u>some</u>/thing	

Phonetic words (but not Dolch):
Note the Vowel Reference Card teams in **bold**.

close /s/	hard	**slow**
dad	lot	thing
dads	lots	time
day	mom	times
dead	moms	zoo
fight	pet	
	pets	

Dolch vocabulary to practice:
Note the Vowel Reference Card teams in **bold**.

a	best	can/not
a/go	big	did
a/head	bird	don't
all	black	**down**
and	boat	**eat**
as	**boy**	**far**
at	**boys**	**farm**
back	brown	fast
be	but	**feet**
bear	by	for
bears	came	from
bear's	can	girl

girls	look	sit
go	may	small
good	may/be	so
got	me	thank
green	my	that
head	no	them
her	not	then
hurt	on	think
I	or	this
if	out	tree
in	play	trees
is	right	try
it	road	up
its	round	was
just	run	went
keep	runs	what
light	saw	when
like	say	will
long	see	with

Black bears _are_ small. Brown bears _are_ big. Black bears can go up trees but so can brown bears. It is not hard for black bears _to_ go up trees for _they_ _are_ small. It is hard for brown bears _to_ go up trees for _they_ _are_ big.

It is best if _you_ don't (_do_ not) **see** a b**ear** at **all** (**may**be in a **zoo**), but if _you_ _do_ **see** a b**ear**, this is what _you_ _could_ _do_. This is what _you_ _should_ _do_. This is what _you_ _would_ _do_! **Right**?

Don't (_do_ not) try _to_ h**ur**t the b**ear**. _You_ _would_ not hurt the b**ear**; the b**ear** _would_ hurt _you_.

Don't (_do_ not) run at the b**ear**. Keep _your_ head d**ow**n. _Do_ not look right at the b**ear's** _eyes_. The b**ear** may think _you_ _want_ _to_ **fight**.

_Do_ not try _to_ _give_ the b**ear** _some_thing _to_ **eat**. Bears can hurt _you_. _They_ _are_ not pets.

Walk. _Do_ not run. Keep _your_ _eyes_ on the bear at **all** times.

If the bear runs at _you_, and _you_ see it is a black bear, sit down and then play dead.

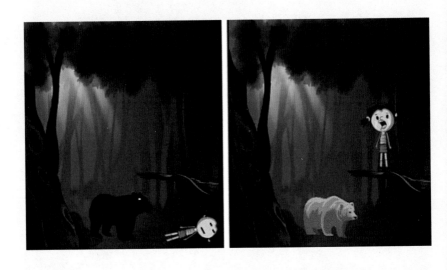

If the bear runs at _you_, and _you_ see it is a brown bear, go up a tree.

One day, not so long ago, I came **out** _of_ my _house_. I _do_ not _live_ in a bird_house_, a boat_house_, a green_house_, a light_house_, a play_house_, a road_house_, **or** a round_house_. I _live_ in a farm_house_. **Bears** _do_ _live_ by my farm_house_.

I came out _of_ my farm_house_. I did _want_ _to_ go **for** a _walk_.

I was not **far** from my farm_house_ when I **saw** a brown bear ahead _of_ me. The brown bear **saw** me and went up on its back **feet**. It was a brown bear, but no_where_ _could_ I **see** a tree _to_ go up.

Was it a mom bear? Was it a dad bear? When _there_ is a small bear with the mom **or** dad bear, the mom **or** dad bear will try _to_ hurt _you_ just so _you_ _could_ not hurt _their_ small bear.

There was not a **tree** by me, but I was close _to_ my farm_house_, so I did _walk_ back _to_ my farm_house_. I did **look** at the bear **all** the time. I did not _walk_ fast. I did a **slow** _walk_.
I did **say**, "**Goo**d bear, **Goo**d bear," lots _of_ times.

The bear did not run at me. "Thank-_you_, Bear!"
Bears can run fast. I cannot run as fast as a bear.

When I got back _to_ the _door_ _of_ my farm_house_, I saw a small brown bear run **out** _of_ the trees. So, I think the big bear was a mom bear. The big brown bear on her back **feet** was the mom _of_ the small brown bear.

I did not run at the big, brown, mom bear. I did not run at the small, brown bear. I did not try _to_ hurt her or her small bear. I did not try _to give_ her or her small bear _some_thing _to_ eat.

So, the **out**_come_ was good. The mom b**ea**r did not run at me **or** hurt me.

I went in_to_ my _house_. I did not go **for** a _walk_ that day.

Bears don't (_do_ not) like moms, dads, boys, **or** girls (maybe _to_ eat), but _they_ will not hurt them if the moms, dads, boys, **or** girls don't (_do_ not) hurt the bears.

Questions to check:

1. Black bears are _____. Brown bears are _____.
   a. big, small
   b. small, big
   c. big, big
2. It is not hard for _____ bears to go up trees for they are _____.
   a. black, small
   b. brown, big
   c. black, big
3. If you see a brown bear, you should _____.
   a. go for a walk
   b. go up a tree
   c. sit down, and play dead
4. If you see a black bear, you should _____.
   a. go up a tree
   b. go for a walk
   c. sit down, and play dead
5. What kind of bear did I see by my farmhouse?
   a. a mom bear
   b. a small, brown bear
   c. a mom bear and a small, brown bear

STORY 2: DOLCH SIGHT WORDS

<u>Where</u> is the Man <u>Who</u> Takes Care <u>of</u> Us?

IMPORTANT: Before studying this vocabulary with your child and before having your child read the story note the following:

This is the first Companion Book to use the Vowel Reference Card words. Up to this point only the non-phonetic Dolch words have been marked in the stories (_underlined and italicized_). Now, however, the Vowel Reference Card teams will be marked in **bold** to help you, parents, help your children spot those vowel teams and **refer them to the Vowel Reference Card** to figure out their sound(s) and therefore be able to read the words.

(Note: The Vowel Reference Card is in the very back of this book!!!)

The single letters a, e, i, o, u, and now also y will not be marked at all as usual. However, parents, for example, if your child sees a single letter o in a word, like in dog, or go, or from, your child needs to be made aware that there are three possible sounds for that letter o (**refer them to the Vowel Reference Card**), not just octopus /ŏ/ as it has been up to this point! This is true for the single letters a (three possible sounds), e (two possible sounds), i (two possible sounds), u (three possible sounds), and y (two possible sounds). Silent e sounds still will not be marked in any way.

COMPANION STORY 39
DOLCH SIGHT WORDS

Non-phonetic Dolch sight words:
(<u>*underlined /italicized as usual*</u>)

<u>could</u>	<u>said</u>	<u>to</u>
<u>do</u>	<u>school</u>	<u>two</u>
<u>horse</u>	<u>some</u>	<u>u/pon</u>
<u>house</u>	<u>some</u>/thing	<u>walk</u>
<u>house</u>/sat	<u>some</u>/time	<u>want</u>
<u>house</u>/sit	<u>some</u>/what	<u>were</u>
<u>live</u> (short i)	<u>some</u>/where	<u>where</u>
<u>of</u>	the	<u>who</u>
<u>once</u>	<u>their</u>	<u>you</u>
<u>one</u>	<u>there</u>	
	<u>they</u>	

Phonetic words (but not Dolch):
Note the Vowel Reference Card teams in **bold**.

care	mile	sat
day	miles	side
glad	miss	still
hair	mom	thing
kid	moms	time
kids	**Moo Moo**	**took**
last	**out**/side	**town**
lot	pond	while
lots	sad	

Non-Phonetic Words:
Baa Baa   la, la, la

Miscellaneous:
1st   2nd   3rd   4th

Dolch vocabulary to practice:
Note the Vowel Reference Card teams in **bold**.

a	drink	it	sit
all	**ea**t	**light**	six
am	**farm**	**light**s	take
an	find	like	takes
and	**for**	long	that
at	**found**	made	them
ate	from	man	then
back	go	me	**three**
barn	g**oo**d	men	**too**
be	grass	not	up
box	had	**now**	us
but	he	old	was
by	here	on	well
cake	hill	**or**	went
cakes	him	**ou**t	what
cow	I	red	will
did	in	**sheep**	with
down	is	sing	with/**out**

Once *upon* a time, *some*time, *somewhere*, *there* *was* an old barn on an old **farm** thr**ee** miles **ou**tside *of* town. *Once* *upon* a time, *some*time, *somewhere*, a man did *live* *there*. He did take care *of* a *horse*, a **c**ow, and thr**ee** sh**ee**p. *They* **all** did like the man.

The man with red hair did like them, but _one_ day the man with red hair was not _there_.

Who will _house_sit while the man is not here?

The _horse_, the **cow**, and the thr**ee** sh**ee**p still did _live_ _there_ in the old b**a**rn on the old f**a**rm thr**ee** miles **ou**tside _of_ t**ow**n. _They_ _house_sat while the man was not _there_. _They_ ate grass and _could_ drink from the box by the well **or** from the pond.

The **cow** _said_, "_Where_ is the man _who_ takes care _of_ us?"

The _horse_ _said_, "_Where_ is the man _who_ takes care _of_ us?"

The thr**ee** sh**ee**p _said_, "_Where_ is the man _who_ takes care _of_ us?"

They **all** _were_ sad. _They_ did miss the man with red h**air**.

One day the _horse_, the cow, and the three sheep went for a _walk_. _They_ did _want_ _to_ find the man with red hair.

They did _walk_ _to_ town. _There_ _were_ lots _of_ men in town, but _they_ did not find _their_ man.

They did _walk_ _to_ a _school_. _There_ _were_ lots _of_ kids in the _school_ and _one_ man, but _they_ did not find _their_ man.

Then _they_ did _walk_ up _one_ hill and down _one_ hill _to_ a farm that was not _their_ farm. _There_ was a man _there_, but he was not _their_ man.

At last, sad, _they_ did _walk_ _to_ _their_ old barn on _their_ old farm three miles **ou**tside _of_ t**ow**n.

Their man with the red hair was _there_!

He had _to_ _do_ _some_thing _somewhere_, and it t**oo**k him a long time.

He was <u>some</u>what sad <u>to</u> go, but **now**, he was back. The man was glad <u>to</u> be back. The <u>horse</u>, and the c**ow**, and the thr**ee** sh**ee**p <u>were</u> glad, **too**.

<u>They</u> made six cakes with l**igh**ts on them. <u>They</u> did sing a lot.

The man with red hair _said_ _to_ the _horse_, the cow, and the three sheep,

"Without me, _you_ did take care _of_ the barn.

You _house_sat for me.

You found grass _to_ eat.

You did drink from the pond.

Good _horse_!

Good cow!

Good sheep!

I am glad I _live_ with _you_. I am glad _you_ _live_ with me."

Questions to check:

1. The old barn and the old farm are _____ miles outside of town.
    a. six
    b. three
    c. two

2. Where did the horse, the cow, and the three sheep walk, 1st, 2nd, 3rd, and 4th?
    a. They did walk to a school, to a farm, to town, to their farm.
    b. They did walk to their farm, to a farm, to a school, to town.
    c. They did walk to town, to a school, to a farm, to their farm.

3. Where did they find their man?
    a. They found their man at their farm.
    b. They found their man at the school.
    c. They found their man in town.

4. Without the man with the red hair, what did the horse, the cow and the three sheep do to live?
    a. They went for a walk.
    b. They found grass to eat and drank from the pond.
    c. They sat down and went to sleep.

STORY 3: DOLCH SIGHT WORDS

The Toy Train

IMPORTANT: Before studying this vocabulary with your child and before having your child read the story note the following:

This is the first Companion Book to use the Vowel Reference Card words. Up to this point only the non-phonetic Dolch words have been marked in the stories (<u>*underlined and italicized*</u>). Now, however, the Vowel Reference Card teams will be marked in **bold** to help you, parents, help your children spot those vowel teams and <u>**refer them to the Vowel Reference Card**</u> to figure out their sound(s) and therefore be able to read the words.

(Note: The Vowel Reference Card is in the very back of this book!!!)

The single letters a, e, i, o, u, and now also y will not be marked at all as usual. However, parents, for example, if your child sees a single letter o in a word, like in dog, or go, or from, your child needs to be made aware that there are three possible sounds for that letter o (<u>**refer them to the Vowel Reference Card**</u>), not just octopus /ŏ/ as it has been up to this point! This is true for the single letters a (three possible sounds), e (two possible sounds), i (two possible sounds), u (three possible sounds), and y (two possible sounds). Silent e sounds still will not be marked in any way.

COMPANION STORY 40
DOLCH SIGHT WORDS

Non-phonetic Dolch sight words:
(_underlined /italicized as usual_)

are	_horse/shoe_	_said_	_watch_
come	_horse/shoes_	_shoe_	_watch_es
_come_s	in/_to_	_shoe_s	_were_
could	_know_	_should_	_who_
_do_	_laugh_	_some_	_work_
full	_laughs_	the	_would_
give	_of_	_there_	_you_
goes	_once_	_they_	
have	_one_	_to_	
horse	_put_	_u/pon_	

Phonetic words (but not Dolch):
Note the Vowel Reference Card teams in **bold**.

fight	in/side	side
fun	lot	smile
glad	lots	time
hard	more	**tow**n
hole	puff	
huff	sat	

Dolch vocabulary to practice:
Note the Vowel Reference Card teams in **bold**.

a	by	**head**/**light**
all	can	**head**/**lights**
an	can/not	help
and	cap	hill
as	caps	I
at	**cold**	in
ball	did	is
balls	don't	it
be	d**own**	its
bear	d**own**	kind
bears	d**own**/hill	let
best	fast	**light**
big	**for**	**lights**
BIG	gave	like
b**ir**d	get	likes
b**oat**	gets	long
b**oats**	g**ir**l	**look**
b**oo**k	g**ir**ls	made
b**oo**ks	go	make
b**oy**	g**oo**d	man
b**oys**	got	much
b**oys'**	had	my
but	has	not
	h**ea**d	

36

now	so	tree
off	start	trees
old	stick	try
on	stick/ball	up
or	stick/balls	us
out	that	use
ride	them	was
right	then	went
run	think	what
say	this	when
see	too	will
snow	top	with
snow/ball	toy	wood
snow/bird	toys	woods
snow/cap	train	
snow/caps	Train	
snow/man	trains	

Once *upon* a time, *there* was an old train. The train did like boys and girls. The train did like glad boys and girls a lot. The train was old, but it was not **too** old *to* *work*. It was not **too** old *to* help.

Once *upon* a time, *there* was a kind, old man with a big smile. The kind, old man likes *to* *laugh*. The kind, old man likes *to* **see** boys and girls *laugh* and smile. The kind, old man likes *to* use old trains that *are* not **too** old *to* *work* and that *are* not **too** old *to* help.

The kind, old man and the train had a *laugh*!

"Let us make _some_ boys and girls _laugh_, **too**," _said_ the old man.

The kind, old man _put_ lots _of_ **toys** on the old train. _Some_ boys and girls help the kind, old man.

There *were* **b**alls, *horseshoes*, **t**oy
b**ears**, *watch*es, stickb**a**lls, b**oo**ks,
toy b**oa**ts, and lots more **toys** on
the train. The train was *full* *of*
toys.

Now the kind, old man, the train,
and the b**oys** and g**irls** *could* be
glad and *have* lots *of* *laughs*.

There, right now, the train _goes_ by a big woods _full_ _of_ trees. _There_, right now, the train _goes_ by a hill.

There, right now, the train _goes_ in_to_ a hole in the hill. The train _put_ its headlights on.

Then the train _comes_ out _of_ the hole in the hill. The train has its headlights off. The train is glad.

The train _goes_ on and on. It is cold. Now _there_ is snow. "_Put_ the toys inside the train," _said_ the old man. A snowbird sat on top _of_ the train.

"It is fun _to_ ride on top _of_ the train," _said_ the snowbird. "I can see so much!"

Look at the **snow**man _some_ **boys** _have_ made. **See** the **boys.** _They_ had a **snow**ball **figh**t by the **snow**man as the **train** went by them. _There_ _goes_ _one_ _of_ the **b**oys' **snow**caps!

Look. _There_ is a **BIG** hill! Can the **train** go up that **BIG** hill?

The **train** will try _to_ go up that big hill. I think the **train** is **too** old.

"What _do_ _you_ think, Train?"

"I think the hill is big, but I don't (_do_ not) think the hill is **too BIG.** I will try my best."

44

What _could_ the train _do_ _to_ get up the BIG hill?

What _should_ the train _do_ _to_ get up the BIG hill?

What _would_ the train _do_ _to_ get up the BIG hill?

The train will **start** and run fast. When the train gets _to_ the hill, the train will try its best. The train will huff and puff.

The **train** will **say**, "I think I can get up this hill." The **train** will **say**, "I think I can get up this BIG hill." The **train** will **say**, "I _know_ I can get up this big hill."

The train got up the BIG, long hill. "Good for _you_, Train. _You_ did it."

"I did it! I did it! I did it!" _said_ the train. "It is not hard, now, _to_ go downhill," _said_ the train. "Now I can _give_ all the toys _to_ the boys and girls and make them _laugh_."

The train went in**to** the **town**.
The **train** gave **all** the **toys** _to_ the
boys and **girls**. **All** _were_ glad. The
snowbird was glad. The kind, old
man was glad. The **train** was glad,
and the **boys** and **girls** _were_ glad.

Questions to check:

1. What was old but not too old to work?
   a. the boys and the girls
   b. the train
   c. the toys
2. Who likes to use old trains that are not too old to work?
   a. the toys
   b. the kind, old man
   c. the boys and girls
3. What did the train say to get up the hill?
   a. "I think I can. I know I can."
   b. "I think the hill is too big."
   c. "I cannot get up the big hill."
4. Is it hard to go uphill or downhill?
   a. uphill
   b. downhill
5. Who were glad?
   a. the hill, the woods, and the hole in the hill
   b. the snowbird; the kind, old man; the train; and the boys and girls
   c. the snowballs, the headlights, and the snowman

STORY 4: DOLCH SIGHT WORDS

Snow

IMPORTANT: Before studying this vocabulary with your child and before having your child read the story note the following:

This is the first Companion Book to use the Vowel Reference Card words. Up to this point only the non-phonetic Dolch words have been marked in the stories (*underlined and italicized*). Now, however, the Vowel Reference Card teams will be marked in **bold** to help you, parents, help your children spot those vowel teams and **refer them to the Vowel Reference Card** to figure out their sound(s) and therefore be able to read the words.

(Note: The Vowel Reference Card is in the very back of this book!!!)

The single letters a, e, i, o, u, and now also y will not be marked at all as usual. However, parents, for example, if your child sees a single letter o in a word, like in dog, or go, or from, your child needs to be made aware that there are three possible sounds for that letter o (**refer them to the Vowel Reference Card**), not just octopus /ŏ/ as it has been up to this point! This is true for the single letters a (three possible sounds), e (two possible sounds), i (two possible sounds), u (three possible sounds), and y (two possible sounds). Silent e sounds still will not be marked in any way.

COMPANION STORY 41
DOLCH SIGHT WORDS

Non-phonetic Dolch sight words:
(_underlined /italicized as usual_)

are	_laughs_	_there_
buy	_of_	_to_
come	_pull_	_want_
could	_put_	_warm_
_do_	_shoe_	_where_
does	_shoes_	_who_
house	_should_	_you_
in/_to_	_some_	_your_
laugh	the	

Phonetic words (but not Dolch):
Note the Vowel Reference Card teams in **bold**.

dad	mom	stove
dads	moms	taste
fat	**out**/side	tastes
fun	pan	te**e**th
glad	pants	time
lot	side	
lots	smile	

Dolch vocabulary to practice:
Note the Vowel Reference Card teams in **bold**.

a	did	**light**	snow
all	don't	like	**snow/man**
am	drink	long	so
an	**eat**	look	stick
and	feet	made	sticks
as	fire	make	store
ask	**first**	man	**street**
at	**for**	**may**	that
back	from	**new**	**too**
barn	girl	not	**toy**
best	girls	now	**toys**
big	good	old	**train**
boy	hand	on	**tree**
boys	hand/made	**or**	**trees**
bring	him	**our**	what
but	hot	**out**	when
can	hurt	play	which
can/not	I	rain	white
clean	in	road	why
coat	is	round	with
coats	it	**see**	
cold	kind	**sleep**	

Come look! _There_ is snow. See
the snow on the road. See the
snow on the street. See the snow
on the trees. See the snow on
our barn.

Where is the rain? I like rain.
Why is _there_ snow and not rain?
There is snow and not rain as it is
too cold for rain now.

Pull on _your_ _warm_ pants. _Put_ _your_ _warm_ _shoes_ on _your_ feet. _Put_ on _your_ _warm_ coats.

Come **ou**tside.

Look back at **our** _house_. **S**ee the snow on **our** _house_.

There is lots _of_ **new** snow. Snow is white. Snow is cold. When snow is cold, it is **light**. When snow is _warm_, it sticks.

I like **rain**, but I like snow, **too**. I like _warm_ snow so I can make a snowman.

Snow is fun. It is fun _to_ play in the snow. It is fun _to_ _laugh_ and play in the snow. I am glad _there_ is snow.

<u>Do</u> <u>you</u> like <u>to</u> **eat** snow? I <u>do</u>, but don't (<u>do</u> not) **eat** it cold. It **may** hurt <u>you</u>. It is goo**d** <u>to</u> make it hot **first** so it is cl**ean**.

<u>You</u> <u>could</u> <u>put</u> the **snow** on a fire **out**side. Make the **snow** hot **for** a long time.

You _could_ bring the snow in_to_ _your_ _house_.

Put it in a pan on the stove.

Make it hot **for** a long time.

Now, _you_ can drink it hot **or** cold.

Now, it is **goo**d and cannot h**ur**t _you_.

Toys may _come_ when _there_ is snow. _Some_ toys _are_ handmade. _Some_ toys _come_ from the store. Moms and dads can _buy_ toys from a store. _Some_ toys _come_ from an old, **toy** train and a kind, old man with a big smile. _Some_ toys _come_ from a round, fat, man _who_ _laughs_ a lot.

_Do_ _you_ ask the round, fat, man _who_ _laughs_ a lot **for** _some_ toys?

_Do_ _you_ _put_ **ou**t a _shoe_ **for** _your_ toys? _Some_ boys and girls _do_ that.

What *do* *you* *put* **ou**t **f**or *your* **t**oys? *Where* *do* *you* *put* it? When *you* sl**ee**p *does* the r**ou**nd, fat, man bring *you* *your* **t**oys? *Does* the r**ou**nd, fat man *who* *laugh*s a lot bring *you* the **t**oys *you* *want* **all** the time?

Does the r**ou**nd, fat man _who_ _laughs_ a lot bring _you_ the **toys** _you_ ask him **for all** the time? Which **toys** did _you_ like the best?

Questions to check:

1. Where is the snow?
   a. The snow is on the road, on the street, on the trees, on our barn, and on our house.
   b. The snow is in our house.
2. When is there snow?
   a. There is snow when it is hot.
   b. There is snow when it is cold.
3. When is snow light?
   a. Snow is light when it is hot.
   b. Snow is light when it is cold.
   c. Snow is light when it is warm.
4. When does snow stick so you could make a snowman?
   a. Snow sticks when it is hot.
   b. Snow sticks when it is cold.
   c. Snow sticks when it is warm.
5. Why should you make snow hot first and then drink it?
   a. You should make snow hot first and then drink it so your teeth don't get too cold.
   b. You should make snow hot first and then drink it so it tastes good.
   c. You should make snow hot first and then drink it so it does not hurt you.

STORY 5: DOLCH SIGHT WORDS

A Boy's and Girl's Show

 IMPORTANT: Before studying this vocabulary with your child and before having your child read the story note the following:

This is the first Companion Book to use the Vowel Reference Card words. Up to this point only the non-phonetic Dolch words have been marked in the stories (_underlined and italicized_). Now, however, the Vowel Reference Card teams will be marked in **bold** to help you, parents, help your children spot those vowel teams and **refer them to the Vowel Reference Card** to figure out their sound(s) and therefore be able to read the words.

(Note: The Vowel Reference Card is in the very back of this book!!!)

The single letters a, e, i, o, u, and now also y will not be marked at all as usual. However, parents, for example, if your child sees a single letter o in a word, like in dog, or go, or from, your child needs to be made aware that there are three possible sounds for that letter o (**refer them to the Vowel Reference Card**), not just octopus /ŏ/ as it has been up to this point!   This is true for the single letters a (three possible sounds), e (two possible sounds), i (two possible sounds), u (three possible sounds), and y (two possible sounds). Silent e sounds still will not be marked in any way.

COMPANION STORY 42
DOLCH SIGHT WORDS

Non-phonetic Dolch sight words:
(_underlined /italicized as usual_)

are	_house_	_some_	_want_
come	_of_	_some/one_	_watch_
_do_	_one_	_some_/thing	_watches_
does	pl**ay**/_house_	the	_where_
done	_please_	_their_	_would_
door	_put_	_there_	_you_
goes	_shoe_	_they_	_your_
have	_shoe_s	_to_	

Phonetic words (but not Dolch):
Note the Vowel Reference Card teams in **bold**.

back/pack	hide	name
back/packs	him/self	pack
b**ar**k	hope	packs
b**ar**ks	kid	self
dad	kid's	thing
dads	mom	things
Dad	Mom	
glad	moms	

67

Dolch vocabulary to practice:
Note the Vowel Reference Card teams in **bold**.

a	don't	hold	show
all	**eat**	I	shows
and	**fall**	in	sit
a/round	**far**	is	**small**
ask	fast	it	**start**
back	**for**	let	take
barn	**for**/get	like	that
be	found	look	these
bed	get	made	**too**
boy	**girl**	must	**toy**
boy's	**girl's**	my	**toys**
but	go	no	up
by	good	not	us
call	grass	**now**	was
can	green	**or**	we
can/not	hand	**our**	what
chair	hand/made	**out**	will
chairs	has	play	with
did	here	round	
dog	him	run	
dog's	his	**see**	

Moms and dads like kid's shows.
Boys and girls like _to_ _do_ shows.
What show _would_ be good?
Let us _do_ a show with **our** dog in the barn!

We _want_ _someone_ _to_ _put_ up a play_house_ for **our** play. Hold it up!
Don't (_do_ not) let it fall! The play_house_ must _have_ a _door_.

Now, *put* it in the barn. *There*.
That is good.

We *are* in the barn. We *want* the playhouse *to* *have* *some* green grass. *Do* we *have* a *watch*, a *shoe*, and a handmade backpack? *Do* we *have* our dog's bed, *some*thing for our dog *to* eat, and our dog's toys?

Don't (<u>do</u> not) **forget** <u>to</u> ask <u>someone</u> <u>to</u> hold **our** dog!

Let us **start** the **show**.

<u>*Please*</u>, <u>*come*</u> and <u>*watch*</u>, Mom and Dad.

Sit here in these chairs.

Girl: Mom and Dad, the name <u>of</u> **our** show is "<u>*Where*</u> is **our** dog?"

Boy: _Where_ is **ou**r dog? I will call **ou**r dog.

"_Come_ here, goo**d** dog. _Come_ here."

(The dog _does_ not _come_.)

Girl: **Our** dog was here, but **now ou**r dog is not in his bed. I will call **ou**r dog.

"_Come_ here, goo**d** dog. _Come_ here."

(The dog _does_ not _come_.)

Boy: My _shoe_ is not here.

Girl: My _watch_ is not here.

Boy: My handmade backpack is not here.

Girl: What has **our** dog _done_?

Boy: Look in the green grass. <u>Do</u> <u>you</u> see my <u>shoe</u> or my handmade backpack? <u>Do</u> <u>you</u> see <u>your</u> <u>watch</u>? <u>Where</u> is **our** dog?

"<u>Come</u> here, goo**d** dog. <u>Come</u> here."

(The dog <u>does</u> not <u>come</u>.)

Girl: Look around the barn. _Do you_ see my _watch_? _Do you_ see _your shoe_ or _your_ handmade backpack? _Where_ is **our** dog? "_Come_ here, good dog. _Come_ here."

(The dog _does_ not _come_.)

Boy: **Our** dog is small. **Our** dog cannot run far. **Our** dog cannot run fast. **Our** dog cannot go **out** _of_ the _door of_ the _house_ by himself.

Girl: Look in the play_house_. _Do you_ see **our** things? _Do you_ see **our** dog?

Boy and Girl: "_Come_ here, good dog. _Come_ here."

(The dog barks.) (The dog _goes_ _to_ the boy.)

Boy: I found **our** dog. I found **our** things. _They_ _are_ **all** here.

They _are_ in back _of_ the _door_ by the play_house_ with _some_thing for our dog _to_ eat. Our dog is here, too.

Girl: Our dog must _want_ _to_ eat with _watch_es, handmade backpacks, and _shoes_. Our dog must _want_ _some_thing _to_ eat in back _of_ the _door_.

Boy: Let us take _your_ _watch_, my _shoe_, and my handmade backpack. Let us _put_ our dog's bed in back _of_ the barn _door_ with _some_thing for our dog _to_ eat. Let us _put_ our dog's toys in back _of_ the _door_, too.

Girl: "Good dog. We are glad you are here with us. We hope you like your bed and your toys in back of the barn door. Here is something for you to eat."
(The dog barks!)

Questions to check:

1. Where will the boy and girl do their show?
   a.   on the grass
   b.   in the house
   c.   in the barn
2. What is the name of the show?
   a.   "Let us look for our dog."
   b.   "Where is our dog?"
   c.   "There is no dog."
3. What things does the dog have with him?
   a.   the playhouse, the door, and something to eat
   b.   the girl's shoe, the boy's watch, and the girl's handmade backpack
   c.   the boy's shoe, the girl's watch, and the boy's handmade backpack
4. Where did the dog hide the shoe, the watch, and the handmade backpack?
   a.   in back of the door by the playhouse
   b.   in the playhouse
   c.   on the grass
5. What did the boy and girl put in back of the barn door for the dog?
   a.   Mom and Dad
   b.   the watch, the shoe, the handmade backpack, the dog's bed, something for the dog to eat, and the dog's toys
   c.   the dog's bed, something for the dog to eat, and the dog's toys

Glossary

Dolch/Sight Words: Words your child should <u>first</u> sound out, using phonics, and then master by sight, so sounding out is no longer necessary.

Phonics: A practice of sounding out words.

Consonants: Sounds, phonemes, which are blocked by the teeth, tongue, and/or lips. Sometimes it is just easier to think of consonants as all the letters that are not vowels: b, c, d, f, g, h, j, k, l, m, n, p, q, r, s, t, v, w, x, y (y can be a vowel or a consonant), and z.

Blends: Two or three consonants next to each other each of which make a sound, such as fl, pr, spr, st, str, and tr. The letter x is considered a blend because it makes the sound /ks/. The letters qu make the sound /kw/ and are also considered a blend.

Digraphs: Two consonants next to each other that make only one sound. The letters ch, sh, th, wh, and ng are digraphs.

Vowels: Sounds, phonemes, which are NOT blocked when pronounced. The vowels are a, e, i, o, u, and sometimes y.

Short Vowels: /ă/ as in apple, /ĕ/ as in elephant or Ed, /ĭ/ as in igloo or itch, /ŏ/ as in octopus, and /ŭ/ as in umbrella or up.

CK Rule: The sound of /k/ can be spelled with c, k, or ck. After a short vowel, the /k/ sound is spelled with a ck.

Floss Rule: The /f/ sound can be spelled with f or ff; the /l/ sound can be spelled with l or ll; the /s/ sound can be spelled with s or ss, and the /z/ sound can be spelled with and s, z or zz. After a short vowel /f/ is spelled ff, /s/ is spelled ss, /l/ is spelled ll, and /z/ is spelled zz. Those two letters (ff, ll, ss, zz) still only make one sound.

Use of s: s is added to nouns and verbs for syntax.

Use of 's: 's is used to indicate possession.

Use of es: To form a plural of a noun, usually add s. However, when a noun ends with s, x, z, ch, or sh, form the plural by adding es.

Silent e Rule: When an e is at the end of a word, it often causes the previous vowel to become long. For example, at becomes ate, mad becomes made, rid becomes ride, and us becomes use. Words such as Mae, lie, doe, and blue can also be considered to be following the Silent e Rule even though there is no consonant between the vowel and the final "silent" e.

Compound Words: A compound word is two or more words, each of which could stand alone, but, also, could be joined together, forming a new word often with a new meaning. Examples of compound words are landslide, milkman, and pancake. Words such as across, alike, and along are also classified as compound words because the **a** (short u (/ŭ/ as in umbrella /ŭ/ or up /ŭ/) as in "Once upon **a** time" can stand alone as a single word, but it can also be joined with cross (across), like (alike), and long (along) to form a compound word. A compound word can be written as a single word (handmade) or as a hyphenated word (first-class).

Vowel Reference Card: The Vowel Reference Card is composed of the most COMMON vowel sounds as found in <u>Remedial Training for Children with Specific Disability in Reading, Spelling, and Penmanship</u> by Anna Gillingham and Bessie W. Stillman, Seventh Edition, Copyright 1960. It does NOT include all the possible ways to say and/or spell those sounds in English.

ABOUT THE AUTHOR/ILLUSTRATOR

Mary Schuler MA, specialized trainer/tutor, is an experienced and result-oriented special education teacher with over 50 years of experience in the special education field. Obtaining her B.A. in elementary education from the College of St. Catherine's in St. Paul, Minnesota, and her M.A. in Special Education, Schuler taught kindergarten, 1st grade, 5th grade, and special education in public school settings. While teaching and tutoring, she discovered that solving learning problems isn't accomplished by just requiring the students to do more schoolwork. She developed/founded the literacy, math, and writing foundational approach resulting in hundreds of students achieving academic and life success. She now works with parent reading coach to train/coach parents/teachers on the literacy, math, and writing foundational approach.

Nicholas Torres MEd, has over 20 years of experience in executive management. He built and led one of the largest and most nationally recognized human services organizations, founded and governed two charter schools, founded a nonprofit focused on scaling high impact social enterprises including school-based health centers and high school/college access and completion pipelines, and founded a social sector consulting organization. Currently, he is president of social innovations partners which publishes the social innovations journal and facilitates the social innovations institute & lab. He serves as adjunct faculty at University of Pennsylvania. He started parent reading coach with his colleagues because he believes parents and caregivers are the primary vehicles toward quality education and should have the educational tools and knowledge to educate their children.

Answer Key

Black and Brown Bears
1. Black bears are **b) small**. Brown bears are **b) big**.
2. It is not hard for **a) black** bears to go up trees for they are **a) small**.
3. If you see a brown bear, you should **b) go up a tree**.
4. If you see a black bear, you should **c) sit down, and play dead**.
5. **c) a mom bear and a small, brown bear**.

Where is the Man Who Takes Care of Us?
1. The old barn and the old farm are **b) three** miles outside of town.
2. **c) They did walk to town, to a school, to a farm, to their farm.**
3. **a) They found their man at their farm.**
4. b) **They found grass to eat and drank from the pond.**

The Toy Train
1. **b) the train**
2. **b) the kind, old man**
3. **a) "I think I can. I know I can."**
4. **a) uphill**
5. **b) the snowbird; the kind, old man; the train; and the boys and girls**

Snow

1. a) The snow is on the road, on the street, on the trees, on our barn, and on our house.
2. b) There is snow when it is cold.
3. b) Snow is light when it is cold.
4. c) Snow sticks when it is warm.
5. c) You should make snow hot first and then drink it so it does not hurt you.

A Boy's and Girl's Show

1. c) in the barn
2. b) "Where is our dog?"
3. c) the boy's shoe, the girl's watch, and the boy's handmade backpack
4. a) in back of the door by the playhouse
5. c) the dog's bed, something for the dog to eat, and the dog's toys

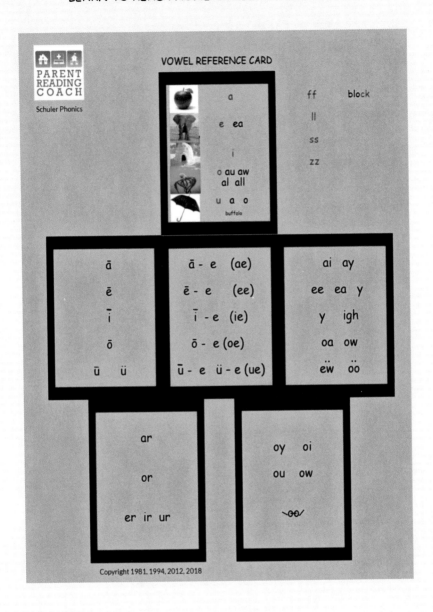

VOWEL REFERENCE CARD

Schuler Phonics

PARENT READING COACH

a

e ea

i

o au aw
al all

u a o

buffalo

ff   block
ll
ss
zz

ā	ā - e (ae)	ai ay
ē	ē - e (ee)	ee ea y
ī	ī - e (ie)	y igh
ō	ō - e (oe)	oa ow
ū ü	ū - e ü - e (ue)	ëw öö

ar

or

er ir ur

oy oi

ou ow

ꞔoo꞊

Made in the USA
Middletown, DE
19 October 2022

12765564R00058